The Renaissance

*A painting of a street scene in crowded Florence,
early in the sixteenth century.
The Renaissance really began in Florence, and many of the best
artists came from there.*

THE RENAISSANCE

by Neil Grant

ILLUSTRATED WITH PHOTOGRAPHS

← A FIRST BOOK →

FRANKLIN WATTS
London and New York

Franklin Watts, Limited,
18, Grosvenor Street,
London, W.1.

Photographs courtesy of:
Albertina, Vienna: page 10
Alinari: page 39
British Museum: pages 21, 23, 31, 65
Giraudon: pages 24, 40, 57, 68
Louvre, Paris: page 73
The Mansell collection: pages 2, 4, 11, 12, 19, 27, 29,
    34, 45, 47, 49, 52, 55, 60, 70, 74
National Gallery of Art, Washington, D.C., Samuel H.
    Kress Collection: page 15
Religious News Service: page 37
Rijksmuseum, Amsterdam: frontispiece

MAPS BY GEORGE BUCTEL

SBN 85166 168 8.
Copyright © 1971 by Franklin Watts, Inc.
Printed in Great Britain by BAS Printers Limited
Wallop, Hampshire

Contents

The Renaissance

I What Was the Renaissance?

Renaissance is a French word, which means "rebirth" or "revival." Historians use it to describe a time in Europe that lasted from about 1450 to about 1550. In those years, great changes were taking place. The Middle Ages were coming to an end, and the Modern Age was beginning.

The changes began with a revival (or "renaissance") of ancient learning. Men studied the writings and the art of the Greeks and Romans, who had lived over a thousand years before. They were astonished by the wisdom of the ancient works, and they were excited by the beauty of Greek art.

The wise men of Greece and Rome had lived before Christian times began. But in the Middle Ages, the Christian Church became the most powerful authority in Europe. Everyone then obeyed the teaching of the Church, and much of the wisdom of antiquity was lost. In the Renaissance, men rediscovered the wisdom and beauty of the ancient Greek world.

First, they copied the Greeks. They made sculptures like the marble statues of antiquity. They wrote the history of their own times in the style used by ancient Greek historians.

Men's interest in the ancient pre-Christian civilization was one important part of the Renaissance.

The duke's palace in Urbino, Italy.
Half palace and half castle, it was built
on the top of a hill and was easy to defend.
Urbino was not a large town, but it was a great centre
for Renaissance artists and scholars in the time
of Duke Federigo de Montefeltro,
who ordered this palace to be built.

Through their study of the ancient world, men came to think more deeply about their own times. They began to ask questions about the world around them. Most of all, they became interested in the study of *Man*: the body and mind of man and everything man had created.

Old beliefs, which had lasted for hundreds of years, were questioned for the first time. Men began to find out new facts, and to discover new places and new ideas.

The new learning was called *humanism*. Humanist scholars studied all the ideas and acts of man (or *humanity*). In the Middle Ages, the Christian Church had not encouraged the study of worldly affairs. But humanist scholars, who had read the works of the Greeks, knew that the Christian Church did not have the answer to every question.

Thanks to the new invention of printing, books could be bought easily ✹ 5 and cheaply during the Renaissance. New ideas travelled much faster than before. A humanist scholar in London knew what his friends in Paris and Rome were writing almost as soon as their books were printed.

Before the end of the sixteenth century, the Renaissance reached every country in Europe. But it began in Italy, and most of the great men of the Renaissance were Italians. It was from Italy that new ideas and new forms of art spread to other countries.

The Renaissance was a time of changing ideas. But ideas change rather slowly. The Renaissance did not start or stop suddenly, like a war. The

The artist Pinturrichio painted this picture
as a record of Pius II entering the cathedral in Siena
after he was elected pope. As well as being head of
the Church, the popes in the Renaissance
were powerful rulers in Italy.

Italian poet Dante, born in 1265, was a Renaissance poet. But William Shakespeare was also a Renaissance poet, and he was born nearly three hundred years after Dante.

All the people described in this book were alive at some time between 1450 and 1550, and most of them were Italians. To find the Renaissance at the height of its glory and excitement, we must look toward Italy in the last half of the fifteenth and the first half of the sixteenth centuries.

II Renaissance Italy

In the fifteenth century, Italy was divided into a number of different states (see the map on page 8).

In the southern half of the country was the kingdom of Naples. Though it was large, Naples was poor, and more backward than the states of northern Italy. It did not play a big part in the Italian Renaissance.

The Papal States, in the centre of the country, were ruled by the pope in Rome. In the north was the republic of Venice, whose capital city was built in a bay, with canals instead of streets. West of Venice lay the duchy of Milan. And in central Italy, next to the Papal States, was the republic of Florence.

Within these four large states were towns and cities, each with its own government. Many towns in the Papal States, for example, were ruled by tyrants who did not obey the pope.

There were also many smaller states in Italy, like the duchy of Modena and the republic of Siena. But they were not so important. The great centres of the Renaissance were Rome, Venice, Milan, and Florence. And the greatest of the four (although it was also the smallest) was Florence.

The Renaissance really began in Florence, and many of the best artists came from there. Later, Rome became the centre of the Renaissance. (But even in Rome, some of the finest buildings and works of art were made by Florentine artists.) When Rome too passed into a less glorious age after 1527, then Venice became for a time the most exciting of the Italian Renaissance cities.

Renaissance Italy

Milan ●
DUCHY
OF MILAN

Verona ● Padua ●
Venice ●

Parma ● Mantua
MANTUA

REPUBLIC

Genoa ●
REP. OF GENOA

MODENA

OF

Ferrara ●
● Bologna

REP. OF
FLORENCE

● Florence

Pisa ●

● Urbino

VENICE

Siena ●

● Assisi

ADRIATIC SEA

REP. OF
SIENA

PAPAL
STATES

REP. OF
GENOA
(CORSICA)

● Rome

KINGDOM
OF
NAPLES

SARDINIA

Naples ●

TYRRHENIAN SEA

MEDITERRANEAN

SEA

SICILY

N

0   50   100   150
Miles

*This is a view of Florence in the nineteenth century.
Even today, it is still a Renaissance city. In the centre
of this picture is the magnificent cathedral, which was taken
as an example by many architects, including Michelangelo.*

This is a painting of a city that never existed.
It shows a Renaissance artist's idea of what a beautiful city
should look like. Renaissance artists were interested
in all *the arts. As you can see, Piero della Francesca*
(who painted this picture) had studied architecture
as well as painting.

11

people slept in the same bed. Their food was simple and their clothes were rough.

Many people kept their own animals. Pigs ran about the city streets, frightening the horses of travellers.

The street was also the city dump. Garbage was thrown from the window, and lay where it fell. It rotted slowly, making a foul black slime.

We think of Renaissance Italy as a place of fine buildings and beautiful art, where rich and clever people lived. But we ought to remember also that many people were not rich and lived in dirty slums.

B

fiercely among themselves. But for the rich and the powerful, life was usually enjoyable and always exciting.

Not everyone was rich. In fact, most people were quite poor. Ordinary citizens in Rome or Florence lived in small crowded houses. Three or four

A German mercenary — a soldier who fought for anyone who paid his wages. This man was a captain, who probably commanded his own private army. It was a dangerous way to earn a living. But mercenaries sometimes lived a long time, because they would run away rather than be killed.

10

The great city-states of Italy were very rich. They lay on the trade route between Europe and the East, and their merchants made large fortunes. The first banks were opened in the north Italian cities in the fifteenth century. The first business companies, which were run like modern corporations, began in Venice and Milan.

The wealthy citizens of the Italian towns wanted to show the world how rich they were. They wanted splendid palaces, with beautiful paintings and fine statues. They wanted their cities to look beautiful too, with spacious squares and grand churches. They had money to pay for such things. They only had to find architects and painters who could build their palaces and paint their pictures.

Such men were easily found. For it happened that Italy in the second half of the fifteenth century was full of great artists.

Why was this so? Why did a state like Florence, which was so small, produce so many artists of genius, all at about the same time? That is a question that no one can truly answer. It was a lucky chance of history.

History often happens like that. A nation that likes singing usually has plenty of good singers. A warlike country often has many good generals. The right kind of men appear when they are needed. So it was in Renaissance Italy. The conditions were right for the creation of great works of art, and there, suddenly, were the artists who could create them.

The princes and rich families of Italy lived well in their beautiful palaces. They admired the works of art around them. They spent pleasant evenings talking about art and literature, while servants kept their glasses filled with wine.

Sometimes their lives were disturbed by war. Sometimes they quarrelled

Map of Italy in Renaissance times.
(The borders of the different states often changed
as a result of wars and treaties.)

III   A Great Patron:
Lorenzo de' Medici

In the fifteenth century, some of the Italian states were republics. They had no prince or king to rule them. Their government was a council and its members were elected.

But the Italian republics were not truly democratic states, because only a few citizens were allowed to vote. Poor men could never be members of the government. Only rich merchants and the heads of powerful families could serve on a governing council.

As time passed, the greatest families gained more power for themselves. Sometimes one man took over the government. When that happened, the state came under the rule of a tyrant, though it often kept the name of republic.

Not all the men who gained power in the Italian states were bad. Some of them were patriotic rulers, whose government was wise and skilful. Many of them were generous patrons of the arts. (A patron is a man who helps artists or scholars, usually by giving them money.)

The Medici of Florence were such men. The citizens of Florence were lucky to be ruled by this family, who governed them well and made their city the most beautiful in Italy.

Like other successful families, the Medici made their fortune in trade and business. They owned the largest bank in Florence. Both the pope and the king of France were customers of the Medici bank.

Soon, the Medici became powerful as well as rich. When Cosimo de'

Medici became head of the family in 1429, he was the most important man in Florence.

But the Medici had enemies in the city. Some people feared that they would become tyrants. Others were jealous of their wealth. In 1433, Cosimo de' Medici and his family were banished from Florence.

People soon found that the government was much worse without the Medici. The next year, Cosimo was asked to return. He entered the city in triumph. The streets were crowded with people cheering and waving. From then on, the power of the Medici was even greater than before.

Cosimo made sure that his enemies would not be able to banish him again. All important posts in the government were given to his friends. The taxes paid by poor men were reduced, but taxes on Cosimo's enemies were increased.

Cosimo himself still had no official position in Florence. He wisely decided to remain a private citizen and to rule from behind the scenes. Yet the government did nothing without his approval, and it always acted on his advice.

Cosimo and his descendants ruled Florence for over fifty continuous years. They were kings in everything except the name.

Florence entered its golden age in the time of Cosimo's grandson Lorenzo, who earned the name "Lorenzo the Magnificent."

Lorenzo was only twenty years old when he became head of the Medici family in 1469. But he had been carefully educated to take over the government, and, as in the case of numerous young men during the Renaissance, he displayed many talents.

Like all the Medici, Lorenzo was a good politician. Thanks to his grandfather, Florence was enjoying a time of peace, and Lorenzo likewise tried to keep out of war. He was not always successful, because in 1474 the pope and the king of Naples joined together against Florence. Then Lorenzo made a daring journey to Naples, where he persuaded the king not to

The hard, clever face of Lorenzo the Magnificent,
who ruled Florence in its greatest age. This bust was made by
Andrea del Verrocchio, the teacher of Leonardo. It is now
in the National Gallery of Art, Washington, D.C.

attack. The pope was not strong enough to fight alone, and Florence was saved.

At home, Lorenzo faced an even greater menace. The danger came from a rival family in Florence, the Pazzi.

If they could get rid of the Medici, said the Pazzi among themselves, *they* would become the most powerful family in Florence. While they kept their jealousy well hidden, they prepared a terrible plot.

The Pazzi planned to murder Lorenzo and his brother, Giuliano, while they were in church for Easter Mass. That Sunday, in 1478, the plotters came to the great cathedral of Florence with daggers under their cloaks. Lorenzo was standing in his usual place near the front, but his brother was not there.

Giuliano had a bad leg, and had decided to stay at home that day. But Francesco Pazzi, leader of the plotters, hurried to the Medici palace and persuaded Giuliano to come to Mass after all. The two young men walked there together, arm in arm, laughing at each other's jokes.

When Giuliano was seated next to his brother, the plotters struck. Suddenly, an armed band surrounded the Medici brothers. The horrified priest at the altar saw knives raised to stab. Giuliano fell at once. Francesco Pazzi, who had been laughing with him ten minutes before, stabbed him eighteen times as he lay on the floor. So furiously did he strike that one thrust of his dagger missed the dying Giuliano and cut open his own leg.

Meanwhile Lorenzo, though he was wounded in the neck, fought his way to a room behind the altar. He locked the door and waited there, with a few friends, until help arrived.

The plot had failed. The people of Florence did not rise against the Medici as the Pazzi had hoped. And Lorenzo took a fierce revenge on the murderers of his brother. The archbishop of Pisa, who had joined the plot, was hanged from a high window. The wounded Francesco Pazzi was dragged through the streets and hanged beside the archbishop. Loyal citizens ran through the city, looking for friends or relatives of the Pazzi. They killed all those they found. Altogether, two hundred and fifty people died in Florence.

After the Pazzi plot, Lorenzo was more popular than before. There were no more plots against the Medici family in his lifetime.

Lorenzo the Magnificent was more than a good statesman. He was a poet, an athlete, and a great patron of writers and artists. His best friends were humanist scholars. At his palace, writers and philosophers met to discuss the problems that concerned them — religion, politics, and literature. Some of them even lived there, but Lorenzo never charged them rent.

Young artists too found a welcome at Lorenzo's court. Sandro Botticelli lived there for a while. He was the first artist since ancient times who made serious studies of the female nude in his painting.

One day Lorenzo met a young sculptor at work on a carving, and stopped to give him some advice. He admired the boy's work and invited him to live at court. This young man was Michelangelo. We shall meet him again.

During Lorenzo's last years, dark clouds were gathering over Florence. The city was no longer as rich as it had been in the days of Cosimo. The years of peace were coming to an end, and foreign armies were preparing to invade northern Italy.

Lorenzo was only forty-three years old when he died in 1492. All Florence mourned his death. Yet within two years, the Medici were banished from the city once more. Many years later they returned again. But by then the golden age of Florence was over.

IV A Renaissance Man: Leonardo da Vinci

Today, when we call someone "a Renaissance man," we mean that he is very talented in several different ways. He may be a statesman who is also a painter, or a poet who is also a successful businessman.

The great artists of the Renaissance were interested in *all* the arts. They were poets as well as painters, and musicians as well as sculptors. Michelangelo used to sign his name, "Michelangelo, sculptor," yet he was also a painter of genius, a brilliant architect, and a fine poet.

But the most amazing brain in Renaissance Italy was the brain of Leonardo da Vinci. There was nothing in the world that did not interest Leonardo, whether it was the wings of a fly or the design of a city. He was a true "Renaissance man." In fact, he was one of the most talented men who has ever lived.

Leonardo was born near Florence in 1452. As a boy, he studied under Verrocchio, the most famous artist in Florence at that time. Verrocchio taught him how to paint and carve in stone. With the other students in Verrocchio's studio, Leonardo made expensive dishes and furniture for rich Florentine citizens.

Before many years had passed, Verrocchio realized that his pupil was already a better artist than he was. There was nothing more that Verrocchio could teach him. At the age of twenty, Leonardo was ready to set up his own studio in Florence.

The city of Florence was then entering its age of glory under its ruling

As a young man Leonardo was very handsome.
But the only self-portrait that we have of him is this splendid drawing
done when he was nearly sixty.

family, the Medici. But though the city was full of artists and other clever men, it did not suit Leonardo.

As we have seen, there were two sides to the revival of learning in Renaissance times: first, the rediscovery of ancient civilization; and second, the discovery of new knowledge about man and nature. Of course, the two sides were not separate, and most people were interested in both.

But in Florence, when Leonardo was a young man, it was the ancient world that held the field. The revival of Greek art was at its height. Scholars eagerly examined the writings of the Greeks and Romans.

Leonardo was more interested in the other side of the Renaissance. He could not speak Greek. Indeed, he was not very well educated. He had no great love for the world of antiquity. He was an inventor, a creator, and a searcher, not a historian.

When he was about thirty, Leonardo left Florence and entered the service of the duke of Milan. In the bustling city of Milan, he soon felt more at home.

Though Milan was a larger city than Florence, it did not have so many fine artists. In fact, Leonardo had no serious rivals there. He was pleased to find that he was treated as a very important person.

Also, the educated citizens of Milan were not so concerned with the works of ancient times. As it happened, the most popular subject in Milan was mathematics, and Leonardo was deeply interested in mathematical problems.

Leonardo's chief task for the duke of Milan was to make a statue of the duke's father. It was to be the largest statue ever made in bronze.

He also put his brilliant mind to work in inventing amusements for the duke's court. He made a mechanical lion for a play, and even designed the actors' clothes as well.

He did not have to work very hard. The bronze statue was never finished. After twenty years in Milan, Leonardo had made only a large model of it.

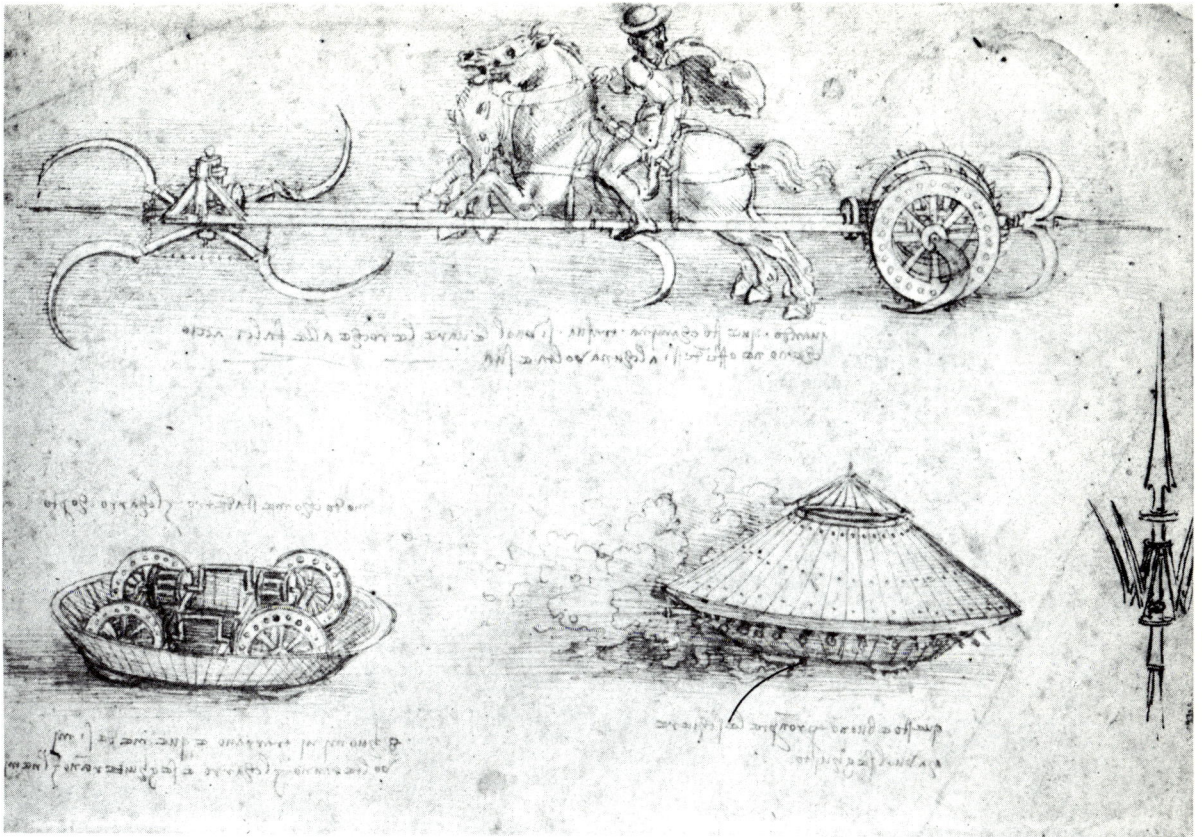

Leonardo designed many war machines.
This is a kind of tank. Inside an iron shell, the tank
was to be driven by horses, or perhaps men. Most of Leonardo's
designs got no further than the drawing board.
So far as we know, no tanks like this were ever built.

Not even the model lasted long. Some soldiers, who wanted to practice their shooting, used it as a target.

Leonardo never accepted what he was told without asking questions. He always wanted to experiment, and to find out how everything worked. He filled many notebooks with drawings of human muscles, or running water, or the leaves of trees.

And he was an inventor. In the fifteenth century, there were no factories and not many machines. Science hardly existed. But Leonardo designed a parachute and a kind of helicopter, and he even planned an automobile that would be driven by springs. Many of his ideas were hundreds of years ahead of their time.

In Milan, he had plenty of time to work out the ideas that came into his amazing mind. He designed huge guns for attacking cities. He invented a way to dam a river. Nothing seemed impossible to Leonardo.

Like many other people, he found that getting up in the morning was hard. So, to wake himself up, he invented an alarm clock, which was worked by water.

Very few of the machines that Leonardo designed were built. And many of them, like his design for a flying machine, would not have worked. But his imagination was astonishing. It is hard to believe that this man lived five hundred years ago. If you read his notebooks, he seems almost like a man of our own times. (If Leonardo *were* alive today, he would probably be planning a colony on Mars, or digging a tunnel under the Pacific.)

Even in his painting, Leonardo was always experimenting. Unlike many other artists of the Renaissance, he never copied. When he painted a subject that other painters had used, he always painted it in a new way.

His most famous portrait, the *Mona Lisa,* is a good example. No other artist had made a portrait like it. No other artist could ever capture the mysterious expression on this young woman's face. Is she smiling or not? It is difficult to say. She seems to be smiling and serious at the same time.

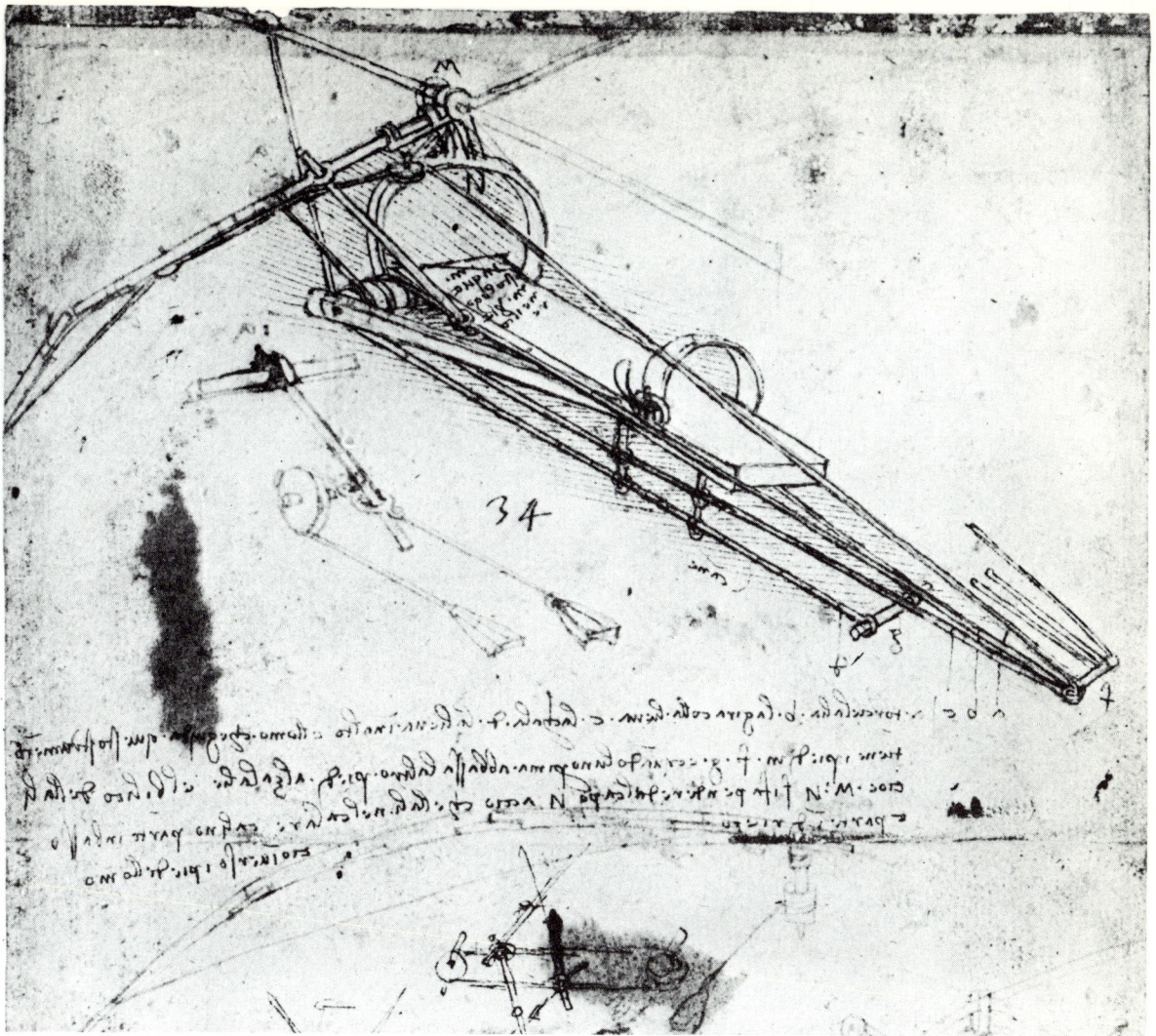

One of Leonardo's flying machines, which looks something
like an ancestor of the helicopter. In this drawing,
you can see some of Leonardo's handwriting.
He used to write backwards — that is, from right to left.
It is easier to read his handwriting when a mirror is held up against it.

Her face has a strange glow, which comes not from her eyes or her mouth, but from her heart.

Leonardo often experimented with different methods and new kinds of paint. Naturally, he made many mistakes. For his wonderful picture of *The Last Supper,* he used a method of painting on wet plaster that he invented himself. It looked splendid when he had finished. But in a few years, dampness came to the surface, and the colours were spoiled.

As a young man, Leonardo wrote, "I wish to work miracles." Such a man was never satisfied with his own work. He always wanted it to be perfect.

We are lucky to have many of his notebooks and drawings today in museums. But Leonardo left very few paintings behind him. Less than twelve still exist, and some of them (like *The Last Supper*) have been badly damaged by time.

In 1499, Milan was captured by the French. Leonardo left the city soon afterward. For the next few years he wandered from place to place. He spent some time in Rome, some in Florence, and some back in Milan. At last the French king Francis I, who was a great admirer of Leonardo's work, invited him to France.

There he spent the last three years of his life, and there, in 1519, he died.

The Mona Lisa, *probably the most famous painting in the world.
No one knows the name of the young lady who posed for Leonardo.
Her mysterious smile is Leonardo's trademark. Most of the women
that he painted, including the Virgin Mary, usually look happy,
not solemn.*

V   Prince and Politician: Cesare Borgia and Machiavelli

Italy was not a peaceful place in the fifteenth century. In every city, great families struggled for power. Sometimes they hired private armies to fight each other. Sometimes they used more simple methods. The dagger and the poisoned drink removed many people from the seats of power.

Family feuds could bring ruin to a town. In the streets of Perugia, for example, men walked with their hands on their swords. For four years, the town was torn by fighting and riots. On one day alone, over a hundred people were hanged in the main square. A nephew of the pope was stabbed to death in broad daylight. The cathedral was used as a camp for soldiers. No one could carry on his trade in such a town, and the citizens of Perugia became poor.

Perugia was one of the worst places for violence and lawlessness. But many other Italian towns lived through times that were almost as bad.

When the citizens of an Italian town were not fighting among themselves, they were usually fighting other people. Every city and state in Renaissance Italy lived on bad terms with its neighbours. Strong states tried to conquer weaker ones. Small states feared larger ones. Wars often broke out, for no state trusted another.

While the country was divided into many different states, each one ruled by a prince or a powerful family, peace and freedom could never come to Italy. Many people knew this was true. But nothing could be done about it then.

The citizens of Florence drove out the Medici family four times. But they always returned.

There was one man who understood this problem very clearly. His name was Niccolò Machiavelli.

Throughout history, many wise men have written books about government and warfare. But none of them has caused so much argument as Machiavelli.

Machiavelli himself once said that politics was the passion of his life.

The sharp-faced Machiavelli. The man who taught
princes how to rule was not a successful politician himself.

c

Many of his forebears had served in the government of Florence. His greatest ambition, when he was a boy, was to follow in their footsteps.

His chance came in 1498, when he was twenty-nine years old. The Medici family had recently been banished, and, for a time, Florence had a democratic government. In this government, Machiavelli was given the important post of vice-chancellor.

For the next few years, he was busy with the affairs of Florence. His job involved mostly paper work, but he also travelled to other countries on government business. He went to France and England, as well as to other states of Italy.

One of these journeys took him to the court of Cesare Borgia, the man who was to be the "hero" of Machiavelli's most famous book.

Cesare Borgia, a natural son of Pope Alexander VI, was the most feared man in Italy. With his father's help, he had set out to make a kingdom for himself in central Italy. In a few years, he conquered a large part of the country.

He worked by violence and cunning. He was a strong man (it was said he could cut off the head of a bull with one stroke of his sword), and he ruled by force. He did not keep his promises when it suited him to break them, and he never trusted other people. He believed only in his own brain and his own army. He even had his brother murdered, because he was jealous of him.

One day, Machiavelli was able to watch Cesare Borgia's methods at work.

The prince had quarrelled with some of the captains in his army. To show that he had forgiven them, he invited them to a banquet. The captains

Cesare Borgia led the papal armies when his father was pope.
He defeated his enemies by murder and treachery, but after
he had conquered, his rule was not unjust.

arrived, and Cesare Borgia greeted them in a friendly way. He invited them to sit down at the table, which was laden with food and drink.

Suddenly, from the shadows, out sprang the soldiers of Cesare Borgia's bodyguard. Daggers flashed in the night air, and the captains fell dead at the table.

Cesare Borgia found it safer to kill his enemies than to forgive them. Why did Machiavelli admire this terrible prince?

Machiavelli believed that the first duty of a ruler was to be successful. Cesare Borgia was certainly that. The ruler must be powerful, said Machiavelli. With regard to his people, he must make them fear him. As stated before, no one in Italy was feared more than Cesare Borgia.

Machiavelli also admired the way Cesare Borgia raised his army.

The armies of Italian states were made up of soldiers who fought only for money. Fighting was their job. They were usually foreigners, who felt no loyalty to the state they were fighting for.

But Cesare Borgia picked his soldiers from his own people. His army, therefore, was loyal to him, and his soldiers fought much harder.

For twelve years, Florence had been trying to capture the nearby city of Pisa, but without success. Then Machiavelli persuaded the government to copy Cesare Borgia's method of raising an army. And when the new army of Florentine citizens went into battle, Pisa soon fell.

Unfortunately, in 1512, Florence had to face a tougher enemy than Pisa. In that year, the Florentines were attacked by a Spanish army — the best in Europe. The Spaniards were too strong even for Florence's new army of citizens, and Florence was defeated.

With the help of the Spanish, the Medici family returned to power. The republic disappeared, and Machiavelli lost his job.

For the rest of his life, Machiavelli spent his time writing. If he had been given the choice, he would rather have worked in the government. Yet it is for his books that we remember him.

NICHOLAS MACHIAVEL'S
PRINCE.
ALSO,
The life of *Castruccio Castracani*
of *Lucca*.

AND

The meanes Duke *Valentine* us'd
to put to death *Vitellozzo Vitelli*, *Oliverotto* of *Fermo*, *Paul*, and the
Duke of *Gravina*.

Tranflated out of *Italian* into *English*;
By *E. D.*

With fome Animadverfions noting
and taxing his errours.

LONDON,
Printed by *R. Bifhop*, for *Wil: Hils*, and
are to be fold by *Daniel Pakeman*
at the figne of the Rainebow
neare the Inner Temple
gate. 1640.

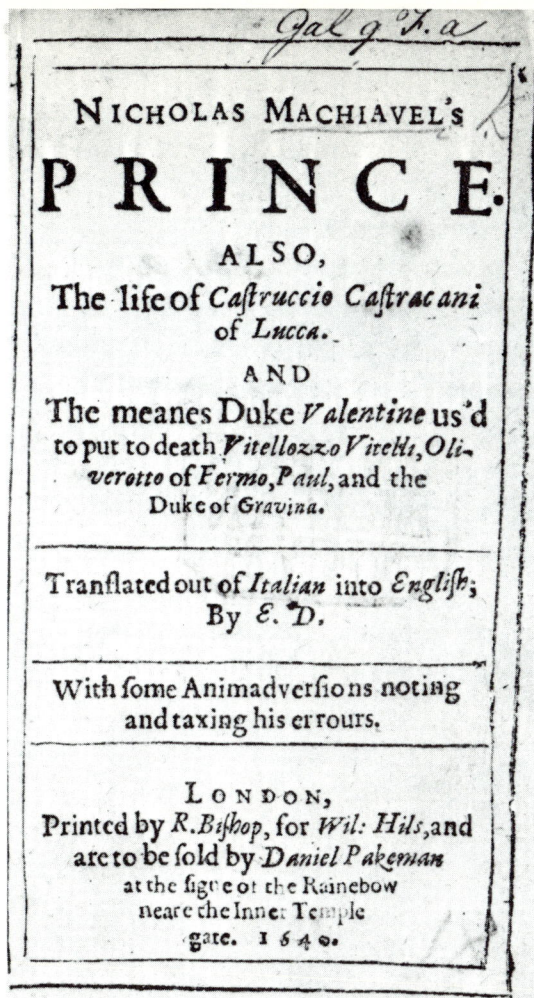

Machiavelli's most famous book,
The Prince, *shocked everybody in Europe.*
It was soon translated into
many languages. This is the
title page of an early English edition.

His most famous work, *The Prince*, is quite short. It is a kind of guidebook on how to be a strong ruler, like Cesare Borgia.

In some ways, *The Prince* is a shocking book. Machiavelli advises the ruler to govern by force and cunning. He may tell lies, commit murder, or do anything at all if it increases his power. According to Machiavelli, honour and goodness are not worth anything.

All men, said Machiavelli, are selfish and dishonest. They cannot be trusted. The prince could not rule by love, because love may easily turn to hate. Therefore he should rule by fear.

The Prince was not wicked so much as realistic. Most Italian princes behaved as badly as Machiavelli advised. He wrote the simple truth about government in Renaissance Italy. But the truth did not make him popular. And the Medici family would not give him his job back, as he had hoped.

Machiavelli would not have been pleased that *The Prince* became his most famous book. He wrote other works about government and history that are much longer. But they do not contain such bold ideas. They are not so shocking, and that is why they are not so well known.

When he was a member of the government, Machiavelli himself never behaved in the way he advised in *The Prince*. He was an honest, decent man, who was not very successful as a politician. He never committed any crimes, and he was a kind husband and father.

So, what did he really believe? Which is the true Machiavelli? The cold-blooded writer who said that all men are selfish liars? Or the hardworking family man? No one really knows. Machiavelli remains a puzzle.

VI   A Great Artist: Michelangelo

In 1503 the government of Florence decided to order two paintings for the walls of the Grand Council Chamber. The paintings were to be very large, and each one was to show a battle scene. Two different artists were hired for this job. The first was Leonardo. The second was Michelangelo Buonarroti.

The two men were fierce rivals. Leonardo already had a great reputation. Michelangelo was much younger, and was challenging Leonardo's position as Florence's finest living artist. Each was determined to create the better picture.

Unfortunately, this exciting contest between the most brilliant men of the Florentine Renaissance was never decided. Neither painting was finished, and nobody can judge who would have been the "winner."

Michelangelo was born near Florence in 1475. He was only fifteen years old when Lorenzo de' Medici noticed his talent as a sculptor. For two years, he lived at the Medici court. Soon after the fall of the Medici in 1494, he made his way to Rome.

During his first visit to Rome, Michelangelo made one of his most famous works. It was the sculpture known as the St. Peter's *Pietà* (the Virgin Mary holding the body of Jesus). This sad and beautiful work, in shining white marble, astonished everyone who saw it. When Michelangelo returned to Florence, he was a famous man. He was still only twenty-six years old.

Princes, bishops, and rich men all over Italy wanted Michelangelo to

work for them. He had far more work than he could finish. Many hopeful patrons were disappointed.

But Michelangelo did make a fine sculpture for his native city at this time. It was a statue of a naked youth, *David* (from the Bible), a magnificent figure fourteen feet tall. It was the finest nude statue that the world had seen since the days of ancient Greece.

The rest of Michelangelo's long life was divided between Florence and Rome. In 1505, he was summoned to Rome by Pope Julius II, who wanted the sculptor to build him a tomb. Michelangelo worked out a plan for a magnificent marble tomb, with about fifty life-size figures carved on it.

He worked on Julius II's tomb for forty years — long after the pope himself was dead. Somehow, nothing ever went right.

First, the pope changed his mind. Then the money ran out. It was difficult to get the right kind of marble. At least five times the plan of the tomb was altered, and each time it got smaller. Michelangelo was in turn bored, tired, and angry. No wonder he complained to a friend that the pope's tomb was "the curse of my life."

When it was finished at last, it was not the grand work that had first been planned. To Michelangelo himself it was a bitter failure.

Even in Renaissance Italy, among so many great artists, Michelangelo stood like a giant. He is one of the true heroes of the history of art. His career lasted throughout the Italian Renaissance (he was nearly ninety when he died). And his influence is still felt by sculptors today.

Michelangelo was not a truly happy man. Few geniuses are. He was

Michelangelo's beautiful Pietà, *in St. Peter's, Rome.*
In 1964, this 450-year-old sculpture was carefully transported
from Rome to New York and put on view at the World's Fair.

never satisfied with his own work, and he could not tolerate anything that was not perfect.

He was a harsh judge of other artists' work, besides his own. He once said that his own servant knew more about sculpture than Leonardo da Vinci did! As a young man, he had some angry quarrels with other young artists. His nose was broken in a fight with the sculptor Torrigiano.

He lived only for his art. He had no time or patience for idle talk. He refused to behave humbly and gratefully toward his patrons. Even the pope sometimes felt the rough edge of Michelangelo's tongue.

A visitor to Michelangelo's studio was amazed to see the sculptor, then aged sixty, attacking a huge block of marble with his hammer and chisel. Chips of stone as big as a man's fist went flying round the room. Yet just one wrong stroke, and the whole thing would have been ruined!

✸

Many of Michelangelo's greatest works were ordered by popes. Paul III put him in charge of the building of St. Peter's, the mother church of the Roman Catholic religion, in Rome. When Michelangelo took over, the building had already been started, and it continued long after his death. But it was Michelangelo who designed the splendid dome, which many architects copied in later years.

Sculptor, painter, and architect, Michelangelo was also a philosopher and a very good poet. He did not divide the arts into separate kinds, as we do, but thought that sculpture, painting, and architecture were all part of the same job. However, he did believe that of all art forms, sculpture was the finest.

Yet Michelangelo's most famous work is not a sculpture. It is a painting.

An overall view from below of the famous ceiling in the Sistine Chapel, painted by Michelangelo.

In 1508 Pope Julius II decided to have the ceiling of his private chapel (called the Sistine Chapel) painted. He persuaded Michelangelo to do it, saying that the artist could choose whatever scenes he liked to paint.

The ceiling of the Sistine Chapel is curved, and it covers an area of over 5,000 square feet. Michelangelo had to paint a picture larger than a basketball court!

A painting on a wall (or ceiling) is called a fresco. The paint must be put on wet plaster. As plaster dries rather quickly, Michelangelo had to work fast.

He divided the ceiling into nine huge paintings of scenes from the Old Testament. Each scene is surrounded by prophets and other figures. Every inch of the ceiling is filled.

Michelangelo attacked this huge task with the energy of a superman. He stood on a wooden platform, sixty-five feet above the floor. As he worked, he had to bend over backward, and for years afterward, he suffered pain in his neck and shoulders. And while he worked in this uncomfortable position, paint dripped onto his face all the time.

Often the pope would come to see how the work was going. Sometimes he climbed the ladder to Michelangelo's platform and asked crossly, "How much longer?" "As soon as I can," was all that Michelangelo would answer.

No other visitors were allowed, but once the painter Raphael, a rival of Michelangelo, crept in to watch. He went away full of wonder and admiration.

Many years after he had finished the Sistine Chapel ceiling, Michelangelo painted this magnificent scene of The Last Judgment *on the wall behind the altar of the chapel.*

This is a detail
of Michelangelo's
Last Judgment.
Notice what terrible
despair the artist has put
into the face
of a man being dragged
by demons into hell.

At last, after four and a half years of backbreaking work, the ceiling was finished. The chapel was opened to the public.

It was a sensation! Everyone knew at once that Michelangelo had made a work of art that might never be equalled. And today, thousands of people go every year to Rome to stand in the Sistine Chapel and gaze up at the result of Michelangelo's genius.

VII   City of the Popes

After the Medici were banished from Florence in 1494, many of the best Florentine artists went to Rome. (Michelangelo was one of them.) Florence was still a lively and exciting place, but its greatest days were passing. In the early sixteenth century, the heart of the Renaissance was no longer in Florence, but in Rome.

In ancient times, Rome had been the capital of an empire. The ancient Romans ruled all the civilized world. Rome was the centre of government, the centre of knowledge, and the centre of art.

Even after the Roman Empire had disappeared, the city of Rome was still the greatest city in western Europe. For it became the headquarters of the Christian Church and the residence of the pope. The Church was very powerful in the Middle Ages. It ruled the lives of every man and woman in Europe. Its laws had to be obeyed, just as much as the laws of states.

For many centuries, Rome was the "capital of Europe." London and Paris were still small towns, built of wood. But Rome, with its grand marble buildings, was called the "Eternal City."

In the fourteenth century, Rome fell on bad times. The pope was forced to leave the city, and had to live for many years in France. Rome had no proper ruler. Battles were fought among the old Roman buildings. Dirt and disease drove the people away.

Early in the fifteenth century, things improved. The pope returned to his palace in the Vatican, and from that day forward, the city began to grow

St. Peter's, Rome. The building of this great cathedral began in 1506, and it was not completed until 1615. Many of the finest artists of the Renaissance were in charge of the building at different times. The great dome, though finished after his death, was built according to Michelangelo's plans.

rich. A hundred years later, it had become once more the greatest city in the world.

The revival of Rome was brought about by the popes of the Renaissance. They did not want to have to flee again to France. So they worked to make their city strong.

Nearly all the Renaissance popes were members of powerful Italian families. They were princes first and priests second. They understood the world of politics very well, and their government was skilful. It was power they wanted, and they knew how to get it.

They were also very rich, because every town in Europe had to pay money to the pope.

In Renaissance times, it was not enough for a ruler to *be* powerful. He had to *show* everyone how powerful he was. Therefore, the popes ordered magnificent buildings and beautiful works of art. They hired the best artists in Italy to make Rome a grand and splendid city.

Like other Italian princes, the popes were also lovers of art. They came from well-educated families, such as the Medici of Florence, and they loved beauty for its own sake, not just as a sign of their power.

The Renaissance popes made Rome beautiful, and they made the papacy strong. But they were not, most of them, good Christians. In fact, one or two of them were not very much better than criminals.

The pope, who is God's representative on earth, should be a holy man. But the Renaissance popes did not often think of God. They were too busy getting more power and money. Though they were not allowed to have wives, most of them had children. They drank too much, they told lies, and they plotted against their enemies.

Of course, not all the Renaissance popes were bad men. And not all of them were princes. Pius II, for example, though he was a nobleman, came from a rather poor family.

Pius did not become a priest until he was 41. But he was elected pope in

D

1458, only twelve years later. Although he had lived a wild and adventurous life when he was a young man, he became more serious after he was elected pope.

He was a wise and tolerant man. And he was honest, which was a rare virtue in Renaissance Italy. Though kind and generous, he did have a sharp tongue. He once described a great cardinal of the Church as "an ugly monkey," and he said the king of Scotland was "small and bad-tempered."

Pius was very intelligent and he had wide interests. In his youth he had won a prize for writing poetry. He was the first of the popes to try to save the ancient buildings of Rome. People did not understand the value of these old ruins, which were the remains of the Roman Empire. Until Pius stopped them, Roman citizens took marble from the ruins to build new houses.

In other ways also, Pius showed that he was a true "Renaissance man." He was an admirer of the beauty of nature. He loved to watch the clouds above the mountains, or the trees reflected in a lake.

Before the Renaissance, no one would have understood such feelings. Clouds were good only because they brought rain for the crops. Lakes were good only because they had fish in them. Nobody thought they were beautiful. Not until the Renaissance did men learn to love the countryside for its beauty.

Pius had faults as well as virtues. Like all the Renaissance popes, he used his office of pope to help his own relatives. He made two of his nephews cardinals. And he gave a palace, which belonged to the papacy, to his sisters.

Pope Pius spent his last years trying to persuade the rulers of Europe to join together in a crusade. In earlier times, many popes had led crusades. Their purpose was to recapture the Holy Land of the Christian religion from the Turks. But Pius failed. The rulers of Europe would not support him, and he died, in 1464, a disappointed man.

If Pius II was the best of the Renaissance popes, then Alexander VI was surely the worst.

Pope Alexander VI as he appears in a fresco (wall painting) in the Vatican, Rome. Despite this picture, Alexander VI did not spend much time praying.

Alexander was elected pope in 1492, and he reigned for eleven years. He was a member of the Borgia family, and his greatest ambition was to make the Borgias the most powerful family in Italy.

He did not care what methods he used. Rivals of the Borgias disappeared mysteriously. Later, their bodies were found in the river. Did the pope have a hand in their deaths? Many people thought he did.

Certainly, the pope's son, Cesare Borgia, was guilty of many murders. Father and son together made the very name of Borgia a sign of terror and cruelty.

The evil acts of the Borgias damaged the papacy too. Who could respect a religious leader who behaved like Alexander VI?

But even the Borgias had some good in them. Cesare Borgia drove out the tyrants who ruled the towns of the Papal States. Perhaps he was not a much better ruler than the men he drove out. But his rule was just, though it was harsh.

Alexander VI was a good politician. He made the papal government stronger, though not more honest. And he brought many fine artists to Rome.

But the pope who added most to the art treasures of Rome was Julius II.

At about the same time that Julius persuaded Michelangelo to paint the ceiling of the Sistine Chapel, he heard of another fine young painter who was working in Florence. This was the great Raphael. He too was soon working for Pope Julius.

Very sensibly, Julius did not tell artists like Raphael or Michelangelo how to paint the pictures that he wanted. He let them choose their own subjects. As Julius had promised, it was Michelangelo, not the pope, who decided what scenes should appear on the ceiling of the Sistine Chapel.

Raphael enjoyed the same freedom. The pope showed him a large chamber in the Vatican palace, and asked him to paint frescoes on the walls.

A portrait of Pope Julius II by Raphael.
(This is a detail from a much larger painting.)
Julius was sixty when he was elected pope. People did not expect him
to live long, but he was pope for ten very lively years.

The result was one of the most beautiful rooms in the world. It still exists, just as Julius II first saw it.

Though he was sixty years old when he was elected pope in 1503, Julius II had the energy of a man of twenty. He was a very tough old man, with fierce eyes and a strong chin. He never felt quite comfortable in his papal robes. He would have made a better general than a priest. In fact, he did once lead the papal army into battle. Even in Renaissance times, such behaviour seemed rather strange for a pope.

The Renaissance popes behaved like ordinary kings or princes, not like leaders of the Christian Church. As a result, the papacy was treated as just another Italian state. It took part in war and made treaties with foreign countries. Naturally, people stopped respecting the pope as a holy man, and Rome became just another capital city, not the very core of the Christian religion.

The Renaissance popes had become politicians and had neglected their religious duties. This was very dangerous. In 1527, Rome paid a terrible price for the popes' mistake.

During the 1520's, Pope Clement VII (a member of the Medici family) quarrelled with the holy Roman emperor, Charles V. The emperor was a dangerous man to quarrel with, because he ruled more than half Europe. He had a large army, which was stationed in northern Italy. Fortunately, he was a good Catholic, and would never have ordered an attack on the pope.

But in 1527, the soldiers of the emperor's army had not been paid their wages for many weeks. They were becoming hard to control. Most of them were German Protestants, who hated the pope and the Roman Catholic Church.

Among themselves, the emperor's soldiers said: "The pope is our master's enemy. Rome is an evil city, but it is surely full of food and wine and money. Let us march there and capture it."

The palace of the powerful Farnese family in Rome.
Though very grand, from outside it looks rather like a prison.
This was not to keep the Farneses in, but to keep their enemies out!

Their generals tried to stop them, but the men would not listen. Like a dangerous wild beast, the huge army began to move toward Rome.

By the time it reached the city, the army had become a mob. The men were half mad with hunger, rage, and envy.

The "Eternal City," in all its Renaissance splendour, lay before them. In a few hours, they had broken through its defences. The Sack of Rome had begun.

For weeks on end, Rome was like a scene from hell. The soldiers rioted in the streets. The pope was captured. Citizens locked themselves indoors, but many were pulled from their houses and killed. Blood and wine ran in the gutters. Smoke and flames rose above the rooftops.

When the terror and violence had ended, Rome was a different place. The joy and brilliance of the Renaissance city had gone forever. It was not ruined, for the great buildings and works of art remained. But the Renaissance in Rome was over.

50

VIII   The Scientists:
Vesalius and Copernicus

In the Middle Ages, men knew very little about science. They knew only what the ancient Greeks had found out. They believed everything that the Greeks had said about science, just as they believed in every single word of the Bible. But the science of the Greeks was very simple, and often wrong.

In Renaissance times, men began to study the world around them, as the Greeks had done so many centuries before. They began to discover new facts. And their discoveries proved that the Greeks had made many mistakes. Old ideas had to be reexamined. New experiments were made. All over Europe, the search for knowledge went on.

We have seen how a man like Leonardo wanted to know how things were made. How did birds fly? Why did falling water always make the same pattern? Leonardo tried to find the answers for such questions.

An artist like Leonardo needed to understand the human body. It is easier to draw an arm or a leg if you know how the muscles and bones are shaped. To help him draw, Leonardo used to dissect (or "cut up") dead bodies to see how they were formed.

It was not difficult to find dead bodies in Renaissance times. The bodies of criminals were left hanging from city walls. People who had died from the plague were left to rot in the street. Anyone who wanted human bodies to study could get them easily.

ANDREAE VESALII.

AN. ÆT. XXVIII

M.D.XLII

Andreas Vesalius dissected human bodies for a different reason. He was not an artist like Leonardo. He was a physician.

Nor was Vesalius an Italian, though he lived in Italy for most of his life. He was born in the country that is now Belgium, and he studied at the University of Paris, in France. He was a very young man when he first became interested in the science of anatomy, the study of how living things are made.

When a man lifted his hand, what was happening inside his arm? How did a man walk, or breathe, or see? What made the human body work? These were questions that Vesalius asked himself.

Vesalius was the first man to study anatomy by dissecting human bodies. A famous Greek physician, called Galen, had explained how he thought the body worked. But Galen had only examined the bodies of animals. Some of his ideas about human anatomy were very peculiar. Vesalius decided to put Galen's ideas to the test.

The results of Vesalius' studies were published in a book called *On the Fabric of the Human Body*. Vesalius was only twenty-five when he began writing it, and he finished it in three years. It explained everything that he had discovered about the parts of the body, the veins, the muscles, and even the brain.

Printing was still a new craft in 1543, when Vesalius' book was published. But it is one of the most famous books ever printed. Not only was it a great advance in human knowledge, but it was also a very beautiful book. The printing was clear and easy to read, and it had nearly three hundred illustrations.

Of course, Vesalius' book did not explain everything about the human

The frontispiece of Vesalius' book about anatomy. It shows
the famous physician holding a human arm that he has dissected.

body. And it had many mistakes. Everyone today knows that the heart pumps blood through the body. But Vesalius did not discover that important fact.

He did show where the veins run and how the heart is made. He even found out a surprising amount about the brain, which doctors today still do not fully understand.

Vesalius was the first man to make a truly scientific study of the human body. He deserves to be called "the father of anatomy."

He wrote other books too. But none of them was so important as *On the Fabric of the Human Body.* After it was published, he became very famous. For many years, he taught anatomy at the University of Padua. Later, he became the personal physician of the holy Roman emperor Charles V. He died at the age of fifty in 1564.

Before Vesalius wrote his famous book, men did not understand how their bodies worked. So it is not surprising that they did not know how the sun, the moon, and the planets worked.

Many people still believed that the earth was flat, like a plate. Nearly everyone thought that the earth was the centre of the universe. The sun and the planets and the moon were supposed to travel round the earth. And the earth itself did not move.

This was the belief of Aristotle, the famous Greek philosopher. And few people ever wondered if Aristotle might be wrong.

One or two men did think differently. Their idea was that the earth and planets travelled round the sun.

Others laughed at this idea. "How silly!" they said. "Anyone who has

Like other great scholars of the Renaissance,
Copernicus was a man of wide learning. He studied medicine
as a young man, he was a doctor of law, and he wrote
a book on how to improve the Polish money system.

NICOLAVS COPERNICVS.

Naturæ novus iste faber fuit. æthera, terras
    Restituit magna cum ratione senex.
Quam calcamus humum, mediis suspendit in astris
    Et Lunæ comites altius ire cupit.
Mercurius priscis migrat de sedibus. ipse
    Immensi medium Cynthius orbis habet.
Hunc circum raptamur et omnis machina mundi.

Immotoque hominum quilibet igne calet.
Inversa est rerum facies. Humana quid ultra
    Mens queat? hic nostri terminus ingenii est.
Cuncta sibi constant. luces noctesque, minoreque
    Est labor. hoc cælos constituisse modo.
Confudit mundum Ptolomæus gentibus. unus
    Hic rerum potuit reddere. quis potior?

Balam.

eyes can *see* that the sun moves round the earth. And if the earth was moving, we should all fall over!"

In the Renaissance, one man proved that this "silly" idea was the right one. His name was Nicolaus Copernicus, and he was born in Poland in 1473. As a young man, he became a priest, but he spent most of his time studying.

If Vesalius was "the father of anatomy," then Copernicus was "the father of astronomy," the study of the stars and planets.

For over thirty years, Copernicus studied all the books that had been written about the universe. There were many different ideas to be looked into. Copernicus was able to prove that many of them were wrong.

It was difficult work, because in those days there were not many scientific instruments to help him. You cannot see very much in the sky without a telescope, but the telescope had not yet been invented.

Copernicus collected all the facts he could find. He compared the writings of different scholars. And, at last, he wrote down his own ideas.

The earth, said Copernicus, is round, and it is turning. Earth and planets move round the sun, just as the moon moves round the earth. The sun, not the earth, is the centre of the solar system.

Copernicus knew that people would find this hard to believe. He tried to explain it as simply as possible. When you sail out to sea in a ship, he said, the land seems to move away from you. Of course, it is the ship that is moving, not the land. In the same way, the sun *seems* to move round the earth. But it is really the earth that is moving.

Copernicus was certain that his ideas were right. But for many years he did not dare to publish them. He knew that people would laugh at him. Still worse, he might get into trouble with the Church. For the Church taught that the earth was the centre of the universe and did not move. And the Church was strict and powerful. It was very dangerous for anyone to

A portrait of a German astronomer with his instruments, painted by Holbein.

say that the Church was wrong, especially if he were a priest like Copernicus.

Only his friends knew what Copernicus believed. But near the end of his life, they persuaded him to publish his ideas. He wrote them in a book called *On the Revolution of Heavenly Bodies.* The first printed copy of the book was put into his hands on the day he died, in 1543.

At first, most people would not believe that Copernicus had discovered the truth. His book was banned by the Church. But other astronomers, like Johannes Kepler in Germany, found that their own studies supported the ideas of Copernicus.

Nearly seventy years after Copernicus' death, the great Italian scientist, Galileo, invented a telescope. For the first time, the movements of the planets could be seen clearly. Galileo proved that Copernicus had been right.

Even then, not everyone believed that the earth really travelled round the sun. Galileo was brought to trial before the pope. He had to swear that he would not teach Copernicus' ideas to his students.

But the Church was fighting a losing battle against science. As more facts about the universe were discovered, everyone at last came to see that the great "Copernican system" was the true explanation.

IX   The Explorers

The world that Europeans knew in the fifteenth century was a small place. It stretched no farther than the coasts of Europe and the Mediterranean Sea. What lay beyond that small area was a mystery.

Some merchants had travelled in Asia, and one or two had gone as far as China. They brought back stories of the great riches they had seen in the Far East. But except for these travellers' tales, the huge continent of Asia was unknown.

To the west lay still greater mysteries. The Atlantic Ocean cut Europe off from the land beyond it. A few bold English fishermen sailed as far as Iceland, but most ships stayed close to the land. No one knew what was on the other side of the grey Atlantic.

Strange tales were told about lands beyond the ocean. There was one country, men said, where the people had two heads! In another place, they had heads like dogs and legs like horses!

During the Renaissance, Europeans began to explore the world for the first time. In 1492, when Columbus sailed, there was only one sea, the Mediterranean, that Europeans knew well. But in the following thirty years, European ships sailed on every ocean in the world.

What caused the voyages of exploration?

At first it was the desire to *find out* (the same desire that Leonardo and Vesalius felt) that sent men out onto unknown seas.

New inventions in shipbuilding made their task easier. Most ships in the Mediterranean were driven by oars. But in the fifteenth century, the first

E

This is a model of Columbus' famous ship, the Santa Maria.
The size of the men in the stern shows what a small ship it was
to cross an unknown ocean.

good sailing ships were built. They could go long distances with only the wind to drive them.

The number of people in Europe was growing. More land was needed. But in the east, the empire of the Turks stopped Europe from expanding in that direction.

The Turks also controlled the trade in silk and spices, which came from the Arab countries and Asia. European merchants hoped to find another trade route for these valuable goods.

Christopher Columbus believed that he could find such a route.

Columbus was born in 1451 in the city of Genoa, which was the greatest seaport in Italy. He first went to sea as a boy, and by the time he was twenty-one, he was captain of his own ship.

He was born with the sea in his blood. He seemed to know when a storm was coming. He could sense shallow water or dangerous currents. His sailors said that he could steer his ship by a drifting cloud or a single star.

When he was still a young man, Columbus had the idea of sailing west to reach Asia. Of course, Asia was east of Europe. But Columbus knew that the world was round. If a ship sailed to the west, he reasoned, it must sooner or later come to the eastern shores of Asia.

His idea made good sense. But there were two problems that Columbus did not know about. First, the world is larger than he guessed. Second, the unknown continents of North and South America block the westward route to Asia.

Columbus needed money before he could test his idea. He tried to persuade the governments of several countries to help him. After many disappointments, he succeeded. The king and queen of Spain promised to give him ships and men.

Altogether, he had three ships, called caravels. They were tough little ships, built of wood, and each one was only about sixty feet long. But they

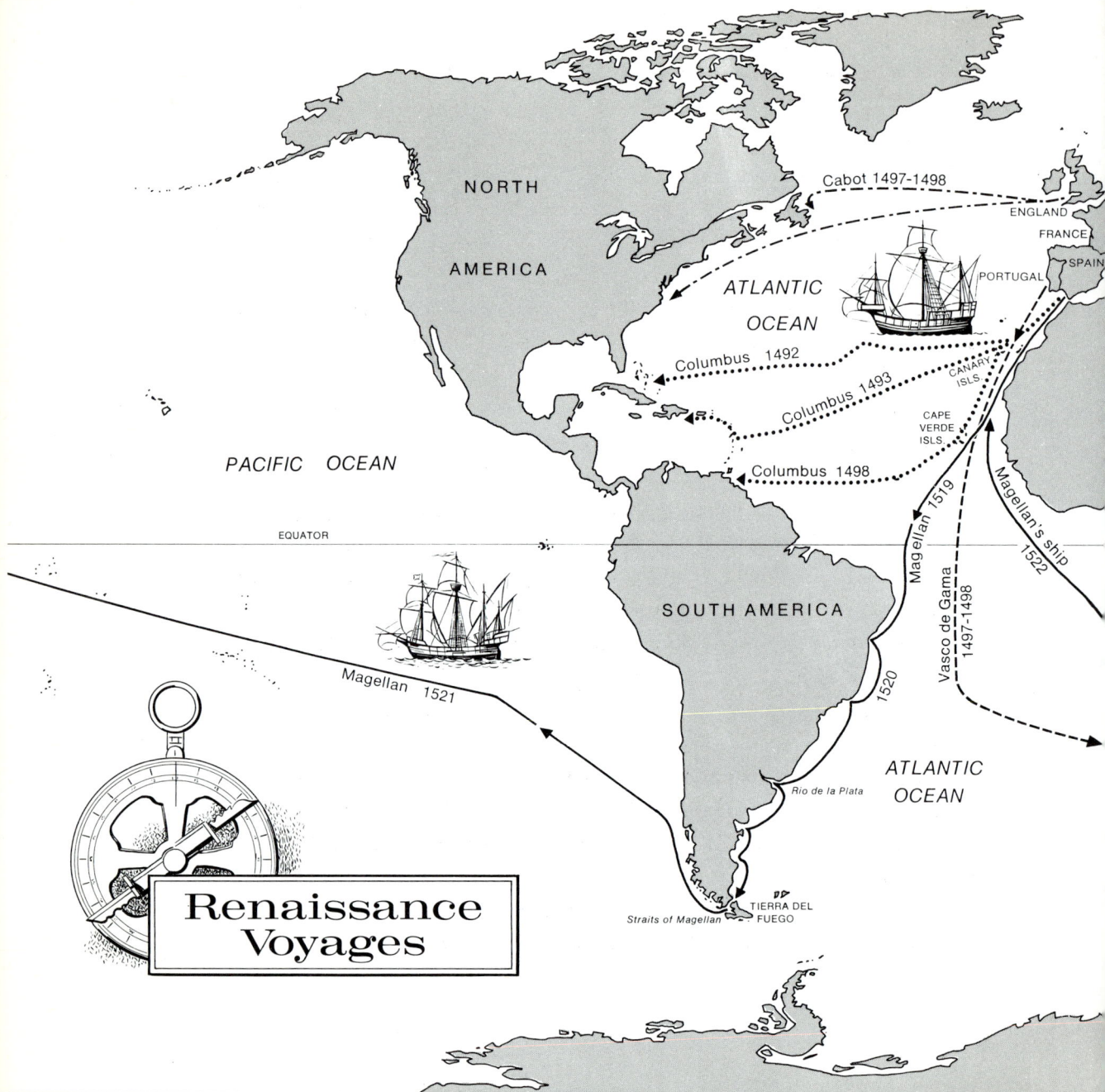

NORTH AMERICA

PACIFIC OCEAN

ATLANTIC OCEAN

Cabot 1497-1498

ENGLAND
FRANCE
PORTUGAL
SPAIN

Columbus 1492

Columbus 1493

Columbus 1498

CANARY ISLS.

CAPE VERDE ISLS.

EQUATOR

Magellan 1519

Vasco de Gama 1497-1498

Magellan's ship 1522

Magellan 1521

SOUTH AMERICA

1520

ATLANTIC OCEAN

Rio de la Plata

Straits of Magellan

TIERRA DEL FUEGO

Renaissance Voyages

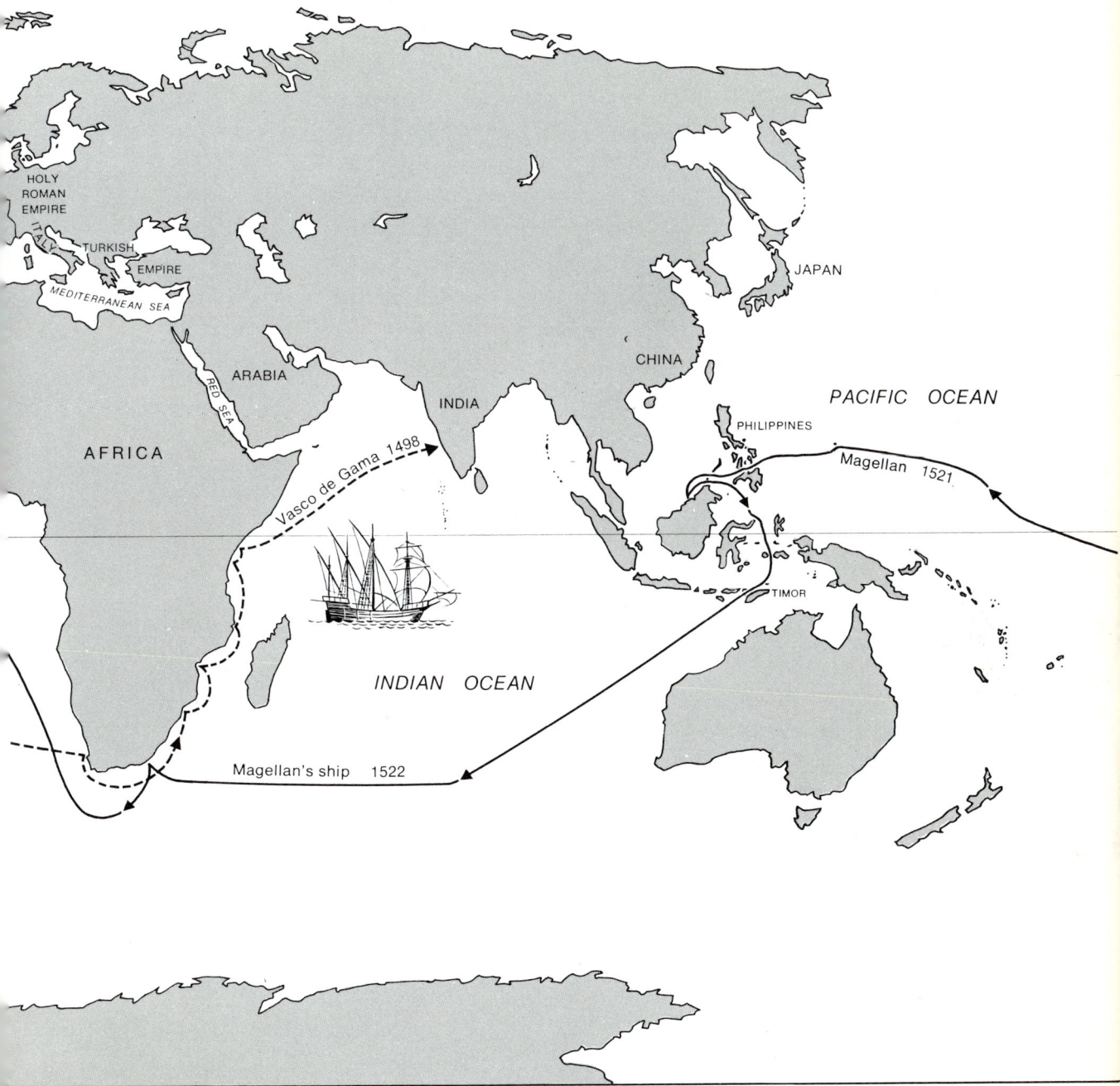

HOLY
ROMAN
EMPIRE
ITALY
TURKISH
EMPIRE
MEDITERRANEAN SEA

JAPAN

CHINA

PACIFIC OCEAN

ARABIA

RED SEA

INDIA

PHILIPPINES

Vasco de Gama 1498

Magellan 1521

AFRICA

INDIAN OCEAN

TIMOR

Magellan's ship 1522

were wide, and would not easily tip up. Each had a crew of twenty or thirty men.

In Columbus' day, there were no good maps. To help him steer the ship, he had no instruments, except a compass. The compass told him what direction he was sailing in, but it could not tell how far he had sailed. His voyage was as brave and as dangerous as a space flight to the moon.

Columbus set out in 1492, and his voyage has become the most famous one in history. He did not find Asia, as he hoped. Instead, he found the New World, the continents of the Americas.

The great captain himself never knew that the land he had come upon was part of a new continent. Though he made three more voyages across the Atlantic, he always believed that the new land was part of Asia. He did not want to discover a new continent! He only wanted to find a sea route to Asia!

Columbus was the first and greatest of the explorers of the Renaissance. But other men soon followed him.

The king of England sent John Cabot to look for the route to Asia in 1497. Like Columbus, Cabot found America in his way. But many Englishmen followed his route and, about a hundred years later, they founded the first colony of English settlers in North America.

Some of the best sailors in the Renaissance came from Portugal. It was a Portuguese, Vasco da Gama, who first sailed round the southern tip of Africa. He pressed on across the Indian Ocean and reached India in 1498. His voyage opened the way for trade between India and Europe.

The most amazing of all Renaissance voyages was that of Ferdinand Magellan.

In 1519, Magellan set out to sail the whole way round the world. It was a daring adventure. He could only guess what dangers he would meet. He could not tell how long the voyage would take. He did not even know if such a voyage was possible.

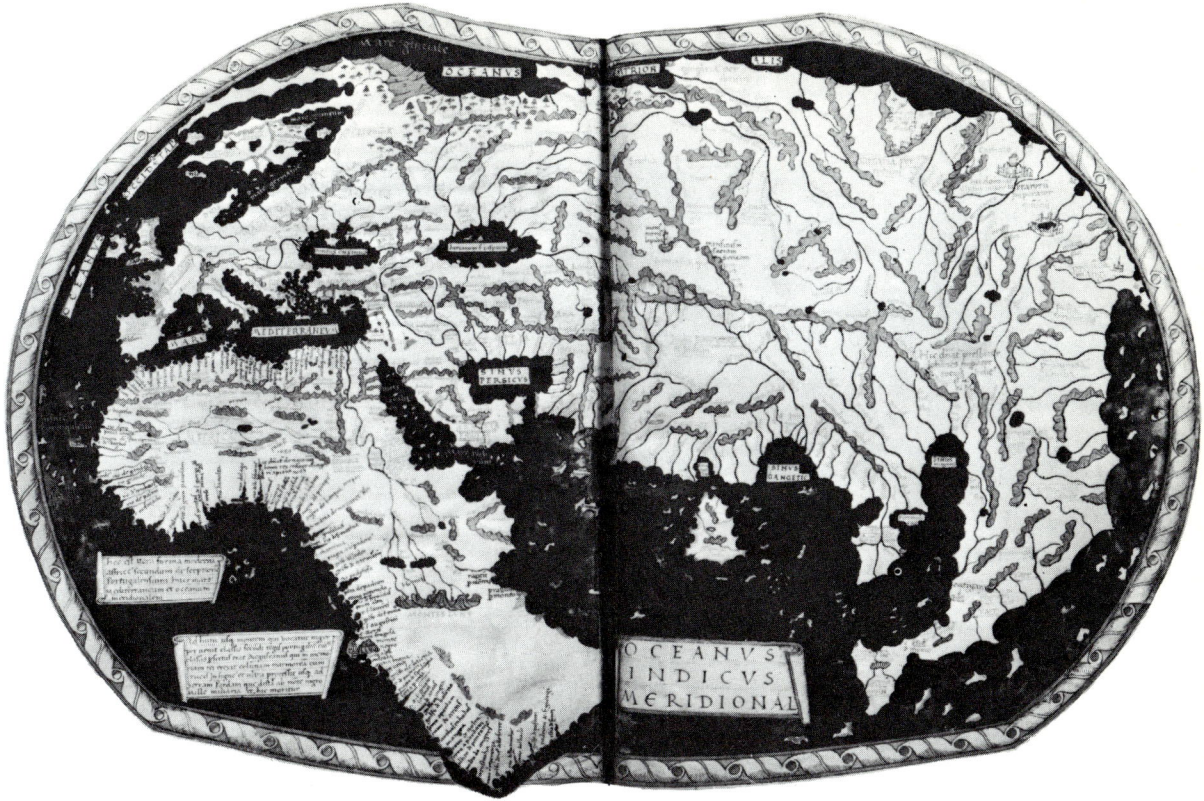

This map was made not long before Columbus reached America.
Except for Europe, the map maker had to guess what the
world looked like.

Magellan and his men lived through storms, shipwreck, wars, and mutiny. In the Pacific Ocean, the food ran out, and the sailors had to boil and eat their own boots.

Most of the crew died. Magellan himself was killed in a battle in the Philippines. But the voyage succeeded.

Three years after they had set out from Spain, twenty-six half-starved sailors brought their battered ship into its home port. They were the only men alive who had circled the globe.

Many years were to pass before another brave captain repeated Magellan's famous voyage. But Magellan had proved that the ships and men of Europe could travel anywhere in the world. Soon, the flags of Spain and Portugal, France and England, were carried to faraway islands and planted on distant shores.

X   Renaissance Europe

The Renaissance reached its full glory in Italy. But it spread to other countries also. By the end of the sixteenth century, every country in Europe had its own Renaissance.

The rest of Europe borrowed many ideas from Italy. Paintings, buildings, and books in northern Europe were influenced by Italian art and literature.

Italian artists went to live in other countries. We have seen how Leonardo went to France when he was an old man. The Florentine sculptor Pietro Torrigiano (the man who broke Michelangelo's nose) worked in England for several years. Other artists went to Spain and Germany and the Netherlands. Even the Kremlin, in Moscow, was partly built by Italians in the fifteenth century.

Italian artists and Italian ideas had an important influence everywhere. But the other countries of Europe had their own traditions too. The Italians did not change everything. Dutch painters in the sixteenth century did not suddenly forget their own style and copy the Italians. They still painted in the Dutch tradition. But if you look at their work, you can see that they had studied Italian art and had learned from it.

The same thing happened in other countries. The beautiful palaces that were built in France in the sixteenth century look a little like the palaces of Italian princes. But they are still very French in style.

Everywhere in Europe, the Italian influence met and mixed with other

*Chambord castle, one of the grandest French
Renaissance palaces. King Francis I had it designed by an Italian architect.
Nearly two thousand men spent twelve years building it.*

traditions. But the results were never the same. The art, the literature, and the music of each country were unique.

Not all the great men of the age were Italians. Flanders (now Belgium) had its own fine painters. France had its own writers. England had many wise humanist scholars.

The greatest philosopher and writer of the age was born not in England, nor in Italy, but in the Netherlands. His name was Erasmus.

Erasmus liked to travel and to visit schools and universities in other countries. For several years he lived in England, and was a friend of the English scholar and martyr Thomas More.

Through his travels, Erasmus met nearly all the wisest men in Europe. He wrote many books. Thanks to the new printing machines, everyone in Europe could learn what Erasmus had said. His name was known everywhere.

Erasmus was a great individualist — a man who said and did what *he* thought was right. He was annoyed by silly customs and bad ideas, and he made fun of them in his books. He was not afraid of attacking the Roman Catholic Church and the pope. As we have seen, the pope was not always a good man, and the teaching of the Church was not always sensible. Erasmus spoke up for common sense and honesty.

Although Erasmus attacked the Church, he lived and died a Roman Catholic. But similar ideas were taken up by Martin Luther, who broke away from the Roman Church and founded the Protestant religion.

The Low Countries (now Belgium and the Netherlands) produced other great men besides Erasmus. Like Italy, the Low Countries had grown rich on trade, and they had a tradition of painting that was almost as fine as Italy's.

Italian artists usually painted important people — popes, princes, and such. But the artists of the Low Countries painted simple folk — peasants at work in the fields, or fishermen selling their catch.

Summer, *a drawing by Pieter Brueghel. Peasants are gathering*
the harvest in a Dutch wheat field. The man on the left
is quenching his thirst with beer.

Erasmus was the greatest man of the Renaissance outside Italy.
His splendid brain alone would have made him famous. But he
was also a very tolerant man, who lived in an intolerant age.
That, and his sense of humour, made him many friends throughout Europe.

In the paintings of a man like Pieter Brueghel, we can see how ordinary people lived in Renaissance times.

An even greater artist than Brueghel was the German painter Albrecht Dürer. He borrowed ideas from the artists of the Low Countries, and after visiting Italy, he began to make use of Italian ideas as well. But even then, Dürer's work remained part of the earlier "Gothic" tradition of German art.

Outside Italy, the Italian Renaissance had its greatest effect in France. After the French armies invaded Italy in 1494, the two countries were in close contact. France held the duchy of Milan for several years, and many works of art were taken from Milan to Paris.

Francis I, who became king of France in 1515, was a great patron of the arts. Leonardo was not the only Italian artist whom the king persuaded to live in France. The Florentine sculptor Benvenuto Cellini spent five years at the French court. Among the works he made for Francis was a magnificent saltcellar of gold and precious stones. When the king first saw it, he cried out in wonder at its beauty — or so Cellini reported.

France was the biggest country in Europe in the sixteenth century. To show their importance, the French nobles wanted splendid castles and palaces. They often employed Italian architects to build them. A traveller in the valley of the Loire today can still see the marvellous results of their work.

The castles of the Loire, like the palaces of the Italian princes, were a sign that Europe was changing. The powerful men who lived in such build-

Albrecht Dürer, a self-portrait as a young man.
The finest painter of the northern Renaissance, Dürer was also
a little vain, as you might guess from this painting.

The famous saltcellar that Benvenuto Cellini made for
King Francis I. The figures represent the sea and the earth.
It is about ten inches tall and is made of gold and
precious stones.

ings were different from their ancestors. They were richer and better educated. They were able to enjoy the good things that their wealth brought them. Theirs was a new way of life.

Europe was no longer a single community, with the pope and the holy Roman emperor as its twin rulers. Powerful new nations had grown up, not only in France, but in England and Spain also. The power of the pope was under attack. The Holy Roman Empire was breaking up.

The people of the Renaissance knew that they were living in an exciting new world. Erasmus wished that he could be young again, to see "the new age dawning." A Frenchman made a list of the discoveries that had been made: "The world sailed round; the largest of the continents discovered; the compass invented; the printing press sowing knowledge; gun powder revolutionizing warfare; ancient manuscripts rescued and scholarship revived; all witness to the triumph of our new age."

He could have added to his list: the growth of trade and new industries; new styles in architecture and the arts; the revival of the theatre and music; the writing of poetry and plays.

In the space of a hundred years or so, man had taken a giant step forward. It had carried him from the Middle Ages, when everything had seemed settled and unchanging, into the Modern Age. As Erasmus recognized, a new world was being born. The Renaissance opened up endless opportunities for the human race. Who could say where human progress would end? It has not ended yet.

Selected Dates of the Renaissance

1464	Death of Pope Pius II
1469	Lorenzo de' Medici comes to power
1478	The Pazzi Plot
1482	Leonardo moves to Milan
1492	Columbus discovers America
	Alexander VI elected pope
1494	The French invade Italy
	The Medici expelled from Florence
1498	Vasco da Gama reaches India
1499	The French capture Milan
1503	Julius II elected pope
	Leonardo paints the *Mona Lisa*
1512	Michelangelo finishes the Sistine Chapel ceiling
1513	Machiavelli writes *The Prince*
1515	Francis I becomes king of France
1519	Death of Leonardo
1519–21	Magellan's voyage round the world
1520	Death of Raphael
1523	Clement VII elected pope
1527	The Sack of Rome
1530	Copernicus finishes his book *On the Revolution of Heavenly Bodies*

1536   Death of Erasmus
1543   Publication of Vesalius' book *On the Fabric of the Human Body*
1564   Death of Michelangelo

Index